Proper Catholic Perspectives

on the Teachings of Luisa Piccarreta

ISBN: 1-891903-35-7

Distributed by:
St. Andrew's Productions
6091 Steubenville Pike, Bldg. 1, Unit #7
McKees Rocks, PA 15136

Tel: 412-787-9735
Fax: 412-787-5024
Web: www.SaintAndrew.com

Printed in the United States of America

Proper Catholic
Perspectives
on the Teachings of Luisa Piccarreta

REV. JOSEPH L. IANNUZZI

St. Andrew's Productions
McKees Rocks, PA

TABLE OF CONTENTS

INTRODUCTION

Devotion to the Divine Will is part and parcel of mankind's millennial quest for union with God. Religions throughout the world embrace a spirituality of union with the Divine Will, and the Catholic Church ascribes to it the greatest achievement of mankind. While devotion to the Divine Will is rooted in Sacred Scripture, Tradition and magisterial teachings, it has become associated in Catholic circles with the writings of an Italian mystic, popularly known as the Servant of God Luisa Piccarreta.

Luisa Piccarreta was born on April 23, 1865 in the small town of Corato, Italy of poor and hardworking parents. Luisa's spiritual journey began while on a farm where she spent many years of her childhood. When she was nine, Luisa received first Holy Communion and Confirmation, and from that moment learned to remain for hours in prayer before the Blessed Sacrament discerning the will of God. Having received only a first grade education, Luisa, at the age of sixteen, received a vision of Jesus. In that vision Jesus asked Luisa to become a "victim soul." This occurred when, from the balcony of her house in Corato, she saw Jesus suffering under the weight of the Cross, who, raising his eyes to her, said: *"Soul, help me!"* From that moment she accepted the state of victim to suffer for Jesus and for the salvation of souls. Gradually Luisa came to experience a most peculiar condition: Every morning she found herself rigid and immobile in bed, with no one able to either raise her arms or move her head or legs. Only the blessing of a priest enabled her to return to her usual tasks of lace making and needlepoint.

On February 2, 1899, Luisa was asked in obedience to her spiritual director Fr. Gennaro di Gennaro to write down the revelations she received from Jesus. These revelations, which she would continue to write until 1938, are popularly referred to as her "diary." Luisa's revelations comprise 36 volumes and contain her intimate and mystical experiences, with dictations from Jesus and Mary on how to "Live in the Divine Will" and hasten its universal reign on earth.

Luisa possessed numerous mystical gifts such as ecstasy, apparitions, visions, the stigmata and bilocation. She was confined to bed with hardly any food or drink except the Eucharist for about 60 years. She occasionally ate and retained other food in very small amounts. Although she was confined to bed, she never suffered any physical illness except for the pneumonia that took her life in 1947.

In 1926 she wrote her autobiography in obedience to her extraordinary spiritual director and confessor St. Hannibal di Francia. St. Hannibal edited her writings, of which the first 19 volumes were properly examined and approved by the local ecclesiastical authorities. He published various writings of Luisa, including the book *L'Orologio della Passione* (*The Hours of the Passion*), which was reprinted four times in Italian.

The Cause of Beatification of the Servant of God Luisa Piccarreta was opened by Rome in 1994 and is still under way. At present, the first 19 of Luisa's 36 volumes bear the local Church authority's *imprimatur* and *nihil obstat*: Luisa's Bishop Joseph Leo and her spiritual director and *censor librorum* St.

Hannibal di Francia, found nothing in her works contrary to the Catholic Faith. However, this does not ensure immunity from error on the part of those who may present or interpret her works in ways that contradict Catholic teaching. For this reason, the Church requests that until the completion and approval of the critical edition of Luisa's collected works, Catholics should exercise caution when reading the translations of her writings (*Pro-manuscripts*) that have been made available to the public in recent years.

As a priest completing a thesis in theology for the Pontifical University of Rome on the correct interpretations of Luisa Piccarreta's writings with the approval of ecclesiastical authorities and the endorsement of G.B. Pichierri, the Archbishop of Trani and head of Luisa's Cause for Beatification, I receive many requests to address errors[1] of modern Divine Will presentations at conferences, retreats and cenacles. I received such requests during my authorized travels to teach and preach the Divine Will in numerous countries and continents.

This thesis that I present to you therefore has one aim: to assist the faithful in the proper interpretation of Luisa's writings.[2] I write this thesis with deep respect for my brother priests and for those laity that are devoted to Luisa, and pray that my words may be received in the spirit in which they are written – a spirit of unity and openness to the truth that Jesus Christ revealed to the Apostles 2,000 years ago.

---

[1]   "Errors" are false teachings that contradict the Church's official teaching office, the Magisterium.

[2]   Luisa's first 19 volumes received the *nihil obstat* by St. Hannibal di Francia, and the *imprimatur* by her bishop H.E. Mons. Joseph Leo.

I recall Jesus' words to Luisa on how He wants these writings made known:

> As I chose Saint Joseph... as cooperator, guardian and vigilant sentry for Me and for the Sovereign Queen, so I have placed beside you the vigilant assistance of My priests as cooperators, guardians and depositaries of the knowledge, the goods and the prodigies that My Will contains. As My Will wants to establish Its Kingdom in the midst of people, so, through you, I want to deposit in My priests this celestial doctrine, as to new apostles. By this means, I will first form in My priests the link with My Will, that they may, in turn, transmit It to the people (June 15, 1926).

Chapter i

Common Errors to Avoid in Presentations on the Divine Will

Let me begin with a litany of early-century heresies and schisms that hindered early Christian communities in their interpretation of the Gospel, which bear striking similarities to many of today's teaching errors on the Divine Will that are too often associated with the writings of Luisa Piccarreta. Again, the sole purpose is of this thesis is, as St. Paul says, to "speak the truth in charity."

1.1 Gnosticism

Of the teaching errors publicly or privately propagated in Christian circles, the primary error puts a new face on the ancient heresy of **Gnosticism**. This heresy is being revived with the following affirmation: "One cannot receive the gift of Living in the Divine Will without access to the secret knowledge contained in Luisa's volumes."

This approach to Luisa's volumes is not sound Catholic doctrine, as many modern mystics received this gift with no knowledge of Luisa's private revelations – e.g., Ss. Faustina Kowlaska, Blessed Dina Bélanger, Ven. Conchita de Armida, et al. (For more information on how God disposes and informs the human intellect to receive the gift of the Divine Will – even before the individual reads Luisa's volumes, so rich in this knowledge – please refer to the Church-approved book, *The Splendor of Creation*, St. Andrew's Productions Pub. [2004] p.142ff – tel. 412-787-9735).

The human creature's ability to receive the gift of Living in the Divine Will without "explicit" knowledge of Luisa's private revelations is analogous to the soul's ability to receive the gift of Baptism. While one cannot place on the same plane as Luisa's private revelations the fruits of the grace of Baptism that formally bring one into the Church, may it serve to simply convey the distinction between implicit and explicit knowledge. The Vatican II Council (*Lumen Gentium*, 16) affirms that while no one can be saved without the gift of Baptism, those who do not have "explicit" knowledge (particular knowledge) of this sacrament, yet live according to the dictates of their conscience by avoiding evil and doing good, are indeed saved through a baptism of *desire*.[3] Likewise, those who do not have "explicit" knowledge of the gift of Living in the Divine Will as contained in Luisa's revelations may indeed receive this gift by *desire*,[4] that

---

[3]   "Those also can attain to salvation who through no fault of their own do not know the Gospel of Christ or His Church, yet sincerely seek God and moved by grace strive by their deeds to do His will as it is known to them through the dictates of conscience. Nor does Divine Providence deny the helps necessary for salvation to those who, without blame on their part, have not yet arrived at an *explicit* knowledge of God and with His grace strive to live a good life. Whatever good or truth is found amongst them is looked upon by the Church as a preparation for the Gospel. She knows that it is given by Him who enlightens all men so that they may finally have life" (*Lumen Gentium*, 16-20).

[4]   Jesus tells Luisa that all that is required to receive the gift of the Divine Will is that the soul desire it with a "firm desire" and "an upright intention."

is, by living in the state of grace and by seeking to live the Will of God in their daily lives.

In my doctoral research of Luisa's doctrines and revelations, I have come to the understanding that the "explicit" knowledge of Luisa's writings enables us tremendously to advance and progress rapidly in degrees in the Divine Will, and the exercise of the Christian virtues enables us to remain anchored in it. But the absence of the "explicit" knowledge of Luisa's revelations does not impede us from receiving this gift.[5] Put simply, *desire* admits, *knowledge* advances, and *virtue* anchors us in the Divine Will!

More needs to be said concerning the supremacy of the mystical gift of Living in the Divine Will as expressed in Luisa Piccarreta's writings. Although many mystics of the past have indeed experienced the heights of union with God's Will, God's mystical gifts remain a gratuitous and inexhaustible offering of Self that God actualizes in the soul of the human creature.

---

5   "While I was thinking about the Holy Divine Will, my sweet Jesus said to me: 'My daughter, to enter into My Will... *the creature does nothing other than remove the pebble of her will...* This is because the pebble of her will impedes My Will from flowing in her... But if the soul removes the pebble of her will, *in that same instant she flows in Me, and I in her.* She discovers all of My goods at her disposition: light, strength, help and all that she desires... It is enough that she desires it, and everything is done!'" (Luisa Piccarreta, *Pro-manuscripts*, Milano, Italy: Associazone del Divin Volere – Casa Editrice di Francesco Gamba, 1977 [this is the only Publishing House on Luisa Piccarreta's writings that is presently authorized by the Archdiocese of Trani], February 16, 1921).

   "To Live in the Divine Will and not know it is absurd, for if one does not know it, it is not a reality but a manner of expression, as the first thing that My Will does is to awaken and to make itself known to those that desire to live together with My Will" (Luisa Piccarreta, Ibid., August 13, 1933).

Below I illustrate the soul's traditional progression in union with God's Will.

1.2 The Human and Divine Modes of Holiness

As the soul matures in its spiritual journey to God, it gradually leaves its human ways of thinking, praying and acting behind (*modo humano*) and enters the divine ways of thinking, acting and praying (*modo divino*). In the writings of St. Teresa of Avila, we find that in its spiritual journey, the soul must pass through seven mansions in order to be divinized and attain to the state of Spiritual Marriage. Noteworthy is the way in which Teresa presents this spiritual evolution. As the soul enters the fourth mansion, its thinking, acting and praying become divine, thus admitting it to the early stages of the *divine mode*, in which it perseveres through the succeeding mansions. As the soul is progressively weaned from its human ways of thinking, acting and praying for itself, its enters the divine ways of thinking, acting and praying for the interests of God and others. It is not until the soul enters the seventh mansion that the divine mode, only by a "special" or "signal grace," divinizes the creature and admits it to the *uninterrupted* and *habitual* participation in God's divine activity.[6] The mystical theologian Fr. Dubay elaborates on the distinction between these two traditional modes:

> How does one pray in the third mansions? Consistently with her whole approach, Teresa says very little about the question, because the prayer is *modo humano*, still somewhat discursive... The last four mansions take up about 70 percent of the text... It is at this stage of development that "the natural is

---

6   St. Teresa of Avila, *The Interior Castle*, translated by the Benedictines of Stanbrook, (IL: Tan Books, 1997), p. 102.

united with the supernatural" and... the mingling between the *human and divine modes* of praying... When God wishes us to give up our *human mode* of praying, He illumines in *His mode* and leads us into an absorption in Himself.[7]

In the seventh mansion, the divine mode becomes continuous. St. Teresa describes God's continuously divine activity in the soul in the advanced stages of the *divine mode*:

St. Teresa's descriptions of this continuous awareness are similar to those of St. John of the Cross. She expresses her mind in several ways: "The soul is almost continuously near His Majesty... *the three divine Persons are very habitually present in my soul... The presence is not merely 'almost continual' but also uninterrupted:* The soul is always aware that it is experiencing this companionship... they have become like two who cannot be separated from one another."[8]

The soul always remains in its centre with its God... the soul itself is never moved from this centre... *they possess him continually in their souls.*[9]

Admittedly, it is only after the Holy Spirit equips the baptized with justifying and sanctifying graces that an additional gift or special grace is required in order that Christ may act divinely in the soul in an habitual and continuous

7   Thomas Dubay, *Fire Within*, (CO: Ignatius Press, 1989), pp. 85-86, 91.

8   Ibid., p.105.

9   St. Teresa of Avila, *The Interior Castle*, translated by the Benedictines of Stanbrook, (IL: Tan Books, 1997), pp. 272-73, 280.

manner. If the soul remains faithful to God's inspirations and graces, it progresses from the *human mode* to the *divine mode* to the *continuously divine mode* of holiness.

1.3 The New and Eternal Mode of Holiness

Up to this point, no mystic has recounted an experience of being so totally absorbed in God as to exert an *"eternal," "continuous"* and *"commensurate"* influence on *"every act"* of every creature. To suppose such an experience would suggest that God should elevate the creature beyond the *continuously divine mode* into his own *eternal mode (modo aeterno)* of operation. But have any mystics in recent times recounted such an experience? The answer is found in the approved writings of the late 19th and 20th century mystics, who describe in full detail God's *eternal mode* in the soul of the human creature. Indeed there were many saints before the 20th century that "experienced" some of the effects of this eternal mode, but, according to their approved works, not in its continuous state.

This is made evident in the writings of the great mystical Doctor St. John of the Cross who reveals that the soul's participation in God's eternal activity, as enjoyed by the blessed in heaven, is *not continuous* in the lofty state of Spiritual Marriage that he enjoyed:

> Even though a soul attains to as lofty a state of perfection in this mortal life as that which we are discussing, it neither can nor does reach the perfect state of glory, although *in a passing way* God might grant it some similar favor... *These experiences are rare.*[10]

---

[10]   "The Living Flame of Love," Saint John of the Cross, *The Collected Works of St. John of the Cross* (Washington, DC: ICS Publications Institute of Carmelite Studies, 1991), translated by Kieran Kavanuagh, O.C.D. and Otilio Rodriguez, O.C.D., stanza, 1, 14-15, p.646.

In another work entitled the *Spiritual Canticle*, John further describes the soul in the state of Spiritual Marriage as *not* possessing as open and manifest a degree of union as that experienced by the blessed in heaven:

> Since the soul in this state of spiritual marriage knows something of the "what," she desires to say something about it… In the transformation that the soul possesses in this life, the same spiration passes from God to the soul and from the soul to God with notable frequency and blissful love, *although not in the open and manifest degree proper to the next life.*[11]

St. Teresa of Avila confirms John's experience:

> In heaven… all love him there and the soul's concern is to love him, nor can it cease to love him because it knows him. And this is how we should love him on earth, though *we cannot do so with the same perfection and continuity*; still, if we knew him, we should love him very differently than the way we do now.[12]

The Servant of God Luisa Piccarreta, on the other hand, sounds the distinctive note of the new mystical indwelling that God has recently imparted to the Church. It is a *continuous participation* in what St. John calls "the perfect state of the glory" that is "proper to the next life." Jesus tells Luisa:

> *The souls that have given themselves completely to Me and that I love, I don't want them to wait to go in the*

---

[11]   Ibid., "The Spiritual Canticle", stanza 39.

[12]   "The Way of Perfection", St. Teresa of Avila (part 1, ch. 30), in *The Liturgy of the Hours* (NY: Catholic Book Pub. Co., 1975), Vol. III, Wednesday of the 13th week, 2nd reading, pp. 431-432.

beatific state when they go to Heaven, I want it to begin
on earth. I want to fill those souls not only with a
Heavenly happiness, but also with the goodness,
sufferings, and virtue that my Humanity had on
earth. I therefore divest them not only of material
desires, but also of the spiritual ones to refill them
with all my goodness, and give them the beginning
of true Beatitude (emphasis added).[13]

The soul who is still wandering unifies herself with
my Will in such a way as to *never separate herself
from It.* Her life is of Heaven, and I receive from
her the same glory that I receive from the Blessed.
Further, *I take more pleasure and satisfaction in her.*
This is because what the Blessed do in Heaven they
do without sacrifice, and with delight.[14]

Luisa relates:

I found myself in Jesus. My little atom swam in
the Eternal Will. Moreover, *since this Eternal Will
is a single Act that contains together all the acts-past,
present, and future, I, being in the Eternal Will, took
part in that single Act which contains all acts, inasmuch
as it is possible for a creature. I even took part in the
acts which do not yet exist, and which must exist, unto
the end of centuries, and as long as God will be God…*
✝ (And Jesus said): "Have you seen what living in
my Will is? It is to disappear. It is to enter into
the ambience of Eternity. *It is to penetrate into the
Omnipotence of the Eternal, into the Uncreated Mind,
and to take part in everything and in each Divine Act*

[13]   Luisa Piccarreta, *Pro-manuscripts* (Milano, Italy: Assocazione del Divin Volere, 1977), Dec. 6 1904.

[14]   Ibid., May 9, 1907.

inasmuch as it is possible for a creature. It is to enjoy, while remaining on earth, all the Divine qualities... It is the Sanctity not yet known, and which I will make known, which will set in place the last ornament, the most beautiful and most brilliant among all the other sanctities, and will be the crown and completion of all the other sanctities (emphasis added)."[15]

I Myself knew how many graces were necessary, having to work the greatest miracle that exists in the world, which is that of *living continuously in My Will*: the soul must assimilate everything of God in its act, so as to give it back again intact, just as the soul assimilated it, and then to assimilate it again.[16]

The approved writings of Blessed Dina Bélanger also affirm the continuously eternal character of the "eternal mode" of mystical union that God has imparted to his Church in recent years:

This morning, I received a special grace that I find difficult to describe. I felt taken up into God, as if in the "eternal mode," that is in *a permanent, unchanging state... I feel I am continually in the presence of the adorable Trinity.* My soul, annihilated in the Heart of the Indivisible unity, contemplates it with greater suavity, in a purer light, and I am more aware of the power that pervades me... Beginning with the grace of last January 25, my soul can dwell in heaven, live there without any backward glance toward earth, and yet continue to animate my material being.[17]

---

[15] Ibid., April 8, 1918.

[16] Idem., Nov 26, 1921.

[17] Blessed Dina Bélanger, *The Autobiography of Blessed Dina* Bélanger, (third edition, 1997), translated by Mary St. Stephen, R.J.M., pp. 219, 227.

My offering is far more active than in the preceding
dwellings where the love of my sovereign Substitute
led me... In this *new divine indwelling*, what strikes
me... is the power, the greatness, the immensity of
God's attributes.[18]

To illustrate that God's eternal mode of activity in the soul
of the human creature is the same interior state enjoyed by the
blessed in heaven–and which St. John of the Cross "experienced
in passing" only—Jesus tells Blessed Dina:

You will not possess me any more completely in
heaven... because I have absorbed you totally.[19]

In dialogue with Jesus, Saint Faustina Kowalska affirms:

The veils of mystery hinder me not at all; *I love You
as do Your chosen ones in heaven*.[20]
My whole being is plunged in You, and *I live Your
divine life as do the elect in heaven*, and the reality of this
life will not cease, though I be laid in the grave.[21]

It is noteworthy that neither Blessed Dina, St. Faustina, or
Venerable Conchita knew anything of Luisa's writings, yet they
all possessed the sublime gift of Living in the Divine Will.

---

[18]   Ibid., p.324, 333.

[19]   Ibid., p. 214.

[20]   Kowalska, St. Maria Faustina, *Diary, Divine Mercy in My Soul*
(Stockbridge, MA: Marians of the Immaculate Conception, 2000), entry
1324.

[21]   Ibid., entry 1393.

That this new, continuously eternal activity brings with it a deeper participation in the activity of the three divine Persons of the Blessed Trinity, is evident in Jesus' words to the Servant of God Luisa and to Venerable Conchita de Armida:

> *All three Divine Persons* descended from Heaven; and then, after a few days, we took possession of your heart and took our *perpetual residence* there. We took the reins of your intelligence, your heart, all of you. Everything you did was an outlet of our creative Will in you. It was a confirmation that *your will was animated by an Eternal Will.*[22] Living in my Will is the apex of sanctity, and it bestows continuous growth in Grace.[23]

> *Do not think that in the mystical incarnation of the Word it is I who act, but the Trinity of the Divine Persons do so*, each one of them operating according to His attributes, the Father, as Father, engendering: the Word as Son, being born; the Holy Spirit making fertile this divine action in the soul.[24]

Also the words of our Blessed Lord to Conchita verify what St. John of the Cross affirmed earlier, namely that the *eternal mode* surpasses the *divine mode* of Spiritual Marriage. When Conchita asked our Lord if the new state she was experiencing was that of Spiritual Marriage as described by Ss. Teresa of Avila and John of the Cross, Jesus reassured her of its supremacy:

---

[22]   Luisa Piccarreta, *Pro-manuscripts*, Vol. I, undated; cf. also Dec 5, 1921.

[23]   Ibid., October 25, 1903; July 18, 1926.

[24]   Marie Michel Philipon, O.P., *Conchita: A Mother's Spiritual Diary* (New York: Alba House, 1978), message of Sept. 22, 1927.

I dare say to him [Jesus]: 'Lord, what you had
promised me, what you had asked of me, was it
(spiritual) marriage... would it be my Jesus, spiritual
✝ marriage? "Much more than that... the grace of
incarnating Me, of Me living and growing in your
soul, never to leave it, of possessing you and of being
possessed by you as in one and the same substance...
is the grace of graces."[25]

The eminent theologian Hans Urs Von Balthasar further
illustrates the new activity of God in the soul of Blessed
Elizabeth of the Trinity, that is unique and unlike the common
life of sanctity in the Church:

Her whole mission is governed by the Third Person,
by the spirituality proper to him, distinct from the
Father and the Son, *rather than by his action through*

---

[25] Marie Michel Philipon, O.P., *Conchita: A Mother's Spiritual Diary* (New
York: Alba House, 1978), p.62. This new gift of mystical incarnation, far
from demeaning the holiness of the state of spiritual marriage, affirms its
nature of ongoing perfection. Fr. Thomas Dubay encounters a statement
by the great mystical Doctor St. John of the Cross, that may at first appear
out of place. In addressing spiritual marriage, St. John states that *"this
communication and manifestation of himself [God] to the soul... is the greatest
possible in this life"* ("Living Flame of Love," John of the Cross, *The Collected
Works*, stanza 3). Fr. Dubay then clarifies this expression by adding, *"one
might think the story must be finished at this point. Not so. The saint goes on to
explain that the person is within the divine splendors and is transformed in them"*
("Fire Within", John of the Cross, *The Collected Works* p.178). Furthermore,
St. John, unlike Blessed Dina Bélanger, writes that while spiritual marriage
confers on the soul a special transformation in this life, it is *"not in the open
and manifest degree proper to the next life"* ("Spiritual Canticle", John of the
Cross, *The Collected Works*, stanza 39, no. 4, p.623). When Blessed Dina
and other contemporary mystics describe their transformation as proper to
the next life, they are reaffirming a new "state," and a perfecting of the state
of spiritual marriage.

the "seven gifts" which is common to all life of sanctity within the Church.[26]

1.4 Elitism

Gnosticism involves **Elitism**, which affirms: "The knowledge of Living in the Divine Will equips the human creature with a new power and superiority that places it above ✝ all other creatures. Hence the creature that lives in the Divine Will is greater in sanctity than all other saints of the past, whose sanctity is inferior to theirs."

This approach to Luisa's volumes is not sound Catholic doctrine, as greatness is determined by the intrinsic nature of the "gift" of the Divine Will itself, and not by the response of the recipient, which God alone beholds. The new and ✝ sublime holiness that we receive from the new gift of the Divine Will does not depend on any novel merit of our own, for it is God who accomplishes this eternal holiness and does everything in us (Phil. 2.13). And if God has prepared for us in heaven a unique mansion for having lived in his Will on earth, it is because He has done it all in us through our simple *Fiat.*

1.5 Montanism

Another common error in the modern Divine Will teaching resembles the ancient heresy of **Montanism.** It can be summed up in the following affirmation: "Because the church hierarchy is unenlightened regarding the sublime gift of Living in the Divine Will, the faithful should submit themselves directly

---

26   Hans Urs Von Balthasar, *Elizabeth of Dijon: An Interpretation of Her Spiritual Mission,* (NY: Pantheon, 1956), p.106.

to the Holy Spirit's revelations to Luisa. The Word of God contained in Luisa's private revelations is the only true authority on this great gift which the unenlightened hierarchy has not yet understood. Furthermore, because the Holy Spirit reveals the gift of Living in the Divine Will through Luisa's revelations, her writings ought to be placed on the same level as Holy Scripture. Therefore, the writings of the Church Fathers, the Councils and the Catholic Catechism are of value to our spiritual growth only insofar as they conform to Luisa's private revelations — not vice-versa.

This approach to Luisa's volumes is not sound Catholic doctrine, as it usurps Scripture's singular role as the normative expression of the fullness of Christ's revelation constituted by the Apostles, to which nothing may be added for all time to come. All private revelations that claim to match Scripture or that contradict Scripture must be rejected as false revelations. Luisa's prophetic revelations add nothing to what Jesus Christ revealed. On the contrary, they explicate Christ's teachings through the activity of the Holy Spirit whom Jesus sent to continue his work of explicating and actualizing the gifts Christ purchased for us, in particular the gift of Living in the Divine Will.

It is our Christian duty from Baptism: to walk humbly with Holy Mother Church, neither lagging behind her (ultra-conservatism), nor running ahead of her (liberalism). Those that adopt the cavalier attitude of placing Luisa's writings on the same level as Sacred Scripture run ahead of the Church (liberalism); and this is the most dangerous road of all. Rather our approach to the Church should be one of filial submission and patience. This was Luisa's approach. Therefore we may prudently encourage others to read Luisa's heavenly volumes in a spirit of filial obedience and docility to the Church's teaching and to her judgment in this matter.

The appropriate Church authorities are preparing a critical edition of Luisa's collected works along with necessary annotations and comments, which may take a good deal of time to complete. Since the Archdiocese of Trani has returned to the Vatican in October 2005 all of Luisa's original writings (including the original volumes it withdrew from the Vatican in 1996), the Vatican will decide whether or not they will be returned to the Archdiocese of Trani. If they are returned to the Archdiocese, it will, in turn, prepare them and release them to the public.

In its official letter of April 15, 2002 and in its official letter to EWTN of August 16, 2003, the Archdiocese of Trani stated that during this interim period pending the publication of Luisa's critical edition, the faithful may draw from sources made lawfully available in print. However, no further printings of her writings are presently allowed without the explicit approval of the archdiocese. This moratorium on printings is effective as of the date of the official letter, August 16, 2003—only the Vatican or the Archbishop of Trani can remove or modify the moratorium.[27]

---

[27]   Articles 9 and 14 of the official letter of August 16, 2003 states: "The Diocese and the Postulation have not permitted nor promoted the printing of her writings since the process is underway and they don't want to create an obstacle in the progress of her cause... The Archdiocese maintains every right to the writings and anything *relative to their printing*. Any violation of these writings will be punished according to the applicable laws."
Note: The words, "the writings and anything *relative to their printing*", refers to Luisa writings that are printed, published and on Internet sites—as devotees may be led to download and "print" the volumes from the Internet sites, which is prohibited as of this official letter dated August 16, 2003.

In June 2005, the Archbishop of Trani H.E. Mons G. B. Pichierri stated publicly that all editions of Luisa's volumes that are available to the public today ("pro-manuscripts") contain "errors." And this is a matter of theological concern to Vatican officials in this period pending her beatification. For such errors have led promoters and devotees, possibly in good faith, to misinterpret Luisa's writings and to publicly spread these misinterpretations at conferences, retreats and cenacles. While the diffusion of Luisa's "pro-manuscripts" is permitted simply to allow the faithful to continue being nourished by her spirituality, only those theologians conversant with Luisa's theology and authorized by the local ecclesiastical authority may instruct the faithful on the correct interpretation of Luisa's writings.

1.6 Quietism

Another modern Divine Will teaching error relates the heresy of **Quietism**, which affirms: "To Live in the Divine Will one must accept all that happens – good, bad or indifferent – as coming directly from the hand of God, and ignore the human instrument that causes the good or the bad, to focus only on the good that may be derived thereof."

This approach to Luisa's volumes is not sound Catholic doctrine, for God created us in solidarity and with human bodies equipped with talents and gifts to be placed at the service of others, for the building up of the Body of Christ. While one must discern the things he can and cannot change, and change the things he can with charity and with holy compassion, he is not exempt from such charitable acts as fraternal correction of the neighbor who has inflicted harm (Mt. 18.15: "If your brother sins against you, go and show him his fault, between you and him alone..."; Gal. 6: "If a person is caught doing something wrong, you who are spiritual instruct such a one in a spirit of meekness…"), or to extend holy gratitude to his neighbor for charity received (Eph. 5.20: "give thanks always for all things…"; 1 Thes. 5.18: "In all things give thanks…"). Quietism replaces the Christian response of charity toward one's neighbor for the sake of his spiritual welfare, with indifference to one's neighbor on the pretext of attaining the heights of holiness – thereby discouraging the human initiative and positive contributions to society. As St. Paul says, we are to "speak the truth in charity" (Eph. 4.15).

1.7 Pietism

Another modern Divine Will teaching error relates to the heresy of **Pietism,** which affirms: "Once you receive the gift of Living in the Divine Will, you are exempt from the need to receive the Sacraments, in particular the Holy Eucharist and Penance. This is because in the Divine Will the soul of the human creature embraces God's one eternal Act, which communicates all that God contains to the soul, including the sacraments and all their effects."

This approach to Luisa's volumes is not sound Catholic doctrine, as it distorts the liturgical and Eucharistic reality of the Church, and denigrates the Real Presence. Otherwise put, the Holy Eucharist is the very God from whom the gift of Living in the Divine Will springs forth, and the human creature cannot receive this gift without the Holy Eucharist. And if the soul is transformed into a living tabernacle, as Luisa states, it is because it's every thought, word and deed are sustained by the power and eternal Act of Christ's Eucharistic reality on earth! To deny the need for the Holy Eucharist is to accept Christ's divinity but to deny his humanity that unites a

Triune communion of Persons to the penitent and the perfect, to the sinner and the saint. No less erroneous is the assertion that in the Divine Will one need not frequent the Sacrament of Penance because the creature ceases to sin altogether. This assertion refutes the teaching of the Councils of Carthage and Trent that condemn the idea of "perfect sinlessness" in this life, and distorts the purpose of the Sacrament of Penance that not only removes sin, but infuses in the soul sanctifying and sacramental graces that positively strengthen it. When Luisa reveals that Living in the Divine Will restores God's likeness to man by the action of the Holy Spirit who takes full possession of the human spirit—so that the inclinations to sin no longer exercise the same "active" psychosomatic influence with the intensity that strained and scarred it in the past – man nonetheless remains free to sin. Apart from the Blessed Virgin Mary, all human creatures, more or less, commit actual *material* sin, even though God's grace may enable them to avoid actual *formal* sin.

1.8 Fideism

Another modern Divine Will teaching error relates to the heresies of **Fideism** and **Esotericism**. These mistakenly exalt private devotions and pious practices above the Church's public devotions and pious traditions. Such modern examples are: the changing of the traditional initials "J.M.J." – representing Jesus (the head of the Church), Mary (the universal mother and patroness of the Church) and Joseph (the universal father and patron of the Church) – with the novel initials "J.M.L." – the "L" representing Luisa.

This approach to the Divine Will and to devotion to Luisa deviates from the Church's traditional practice, inasmuch as it usurps St. Joseph's role of universal father and patron of the Church by placing Luisa in his stead. In point of fact, since 1870 the Church officially confirmed the great dignity of St. Joseph when Blessed Pope Pius IX declared St. Joseph Patron of the Universal Church, and when Pope Leo XIII set St. Joseph before us with a rank and place best described in his encyclical *Quamquam Pluries*, 1889:

> "The special motives for which St. Joseph has been proclaimed Patron of the Church, and from which the Church looks for *singular* benefit from his patronage and protection, are that Joseph was the spouse of Mary and that he was reputed the Father of Jesus Christ. From these sources have sprung his *dignity*, his *holiness*, his *glory*... But as Joseph has been united to the Blessed Virgin by the ties of marriage, *it may not be doubted that he approached nearer than any other creature the supreminent dignity* by which the Mother of God surpasses so nobly all created natures."

It is important to distinguish between the encyclical terms of "dignity" and "holiness." While Luisa cannot match the "dignity" of the offices of mother and putative father that Mary and Joseph perfectly fulfilled, Jesus assures Luisa that the new gift of continuous participation in his eternal "holiness" that he imparted to her can indeed excel all other gifts of holiness that he imparted to other creatures before her, save Mary.

Jesus reveals to Luisa that St. Joseph experienced the "effects" of this new gift of holiness that she possessed in view of its full actualization in Mary and in her. It is no wonder that in heaven both "dignity" and "holiness" constitute our eternal reward. In heaven we will be rewarded both for having faithfully fulfilled the office that God has given to us in this life (dignity), and for having faithfully corresponded to whatever sanctifying graces God deigned to grant us in this life (holiness). Thus the dignity of Luisa's office as the "little daughter of the Divine Will", or as the secretary of the Holy Spirit's Fiat of Sanctification, does not supersede the dignity of St. Joseph's office of father of Jesus. But the new gift of the eternal holiness that God communicated to Mary, to Luisa and to all souls after these for the good of the Church, raises them to the new and continuous plane of God's *eternal mode*, which supersedes all previous states of mystical union (*Nota bene*: The Blessed Virgin Mary enjoyed this state of mystical union - *Living in the Divine Will* – to a degree that no human creature can ever attain by virtue of her Immaculate Conception, her perpetual virginity, her office of Mother of God and her fidelity to the Will of God. For more information on the continuous participation in the *eternal mode* of holiness, I refer you to the Church-approved book, *The Splendor of Creation*, St. Andrew Productions [2004] cf. chapter 3.5).

1.9 Luisa and Mary

Another erroneous teaching places Luisa on the same level of holiness and maternity as Blessed Mary, the Mother of God.

This kind of devotion to Luisa is not sound Catholic doctrine, as no creature conceived with original sin can ever match Mary's holiness, nor can anyone equal the dignity of her singular office of universal and divine mother. Certainly, we can "participate" in Mary's office of universal mother, inasmuch as we too can influence the lives of every act of every creature like Mary, through Mary, but never can we or Luisa ever match her degree of union with the Divine Will – a degree of union that she helped communicate to Luisa and that she helps to communicate to us.

1.10 Luisa and Sainthood

Another teaching error affirms that Living in the Divine Will is greater and more exalted than sainthood.

This affirmation is inconsistent with the Church's traditional teaching on sainthood, which is the attainment of heroic virtue and the beatitudes in this life. While this attainment may differ in degrees, the Church regards sainthood as the participation on earth in the divine and eternal life of God. Living in the Divine Will is the "continuous" participation in the eternal life of God. The Church has taught since time immemorial that the only step toward God beyond sainthood is that of the "beatific vision" or "beatific mode" that the saints enjoy in heaven. Those that live in the Divine Will on earth do not experience the beatific vision or mode, but the "eternal mode" that admits them to the continuous participation in God's eternal activity (for more information on the distinction between the eternal and beatific modes, I refer you to the Church-approved publication entitled, *The Splendor of Creation*, St. Andrew's Productions, 2004).

1.11 Divine Holiness

Another controversial teaching affirms: "That which makes Luisa's gift of holiness new is a *Divine* holiness."

While the gift Luisa describes of Living in the Divine Will is indeed new, one ought not identify it exclusively as a "divine" holiness. All the baptized enjoy a divine holiness, and for this reason, divine holiness is not new. Rather, the new trait of living in God's Will is God's sublimation of his divine activity in the soul of the baptized to his *continuously eternal* activity.

Living in the Divine Will is not simply a divine holiness; it is an *eternal holiness* that imparts to us the fullness of the divine life. Living in the Divine Will is described in the writings of Luisa as the creature's participation on earth in God's *new, eternal holiness* that the Blessed enjoy in heaven. It is heaven on earth internalized! The Church has always offered to the faithful a divine sanctity, and in recent years she has received a greater outpouring of this sanctity by virtue of God's continuously eternal activity' within the soul of the human creature.

1.12 Palagenism

Related to the exclusively divine holiness, is the assertion that the saints of the past possessed merely a "human holiness."

This assertion puts a new face on the ancient heresy of is **Palagenism.** The advocates of this ancient heresy affirm that since all saints of the past did not receive the gift of Living in the Divine Will, they achieved holiness primarily or exclusively by human means. In contrast to this assertion, the Church affirms that the holiness of past saints is not primarily the fruit of human achievement, but it is primarily the fruit of God's divine grace at work in the soul of the human creature. The Apostles, the Church Fathers, the Doctors and the mystics have consistently taught that Baptism, wrought by Christ's Incarnation, Passion, death and Resurrection, confers upon the baptized the indwelling of the Holy Spirit, who expels original sin and infuses within it faith, hope and love. Hence the baptized becomes a "new" creature in Christ, a partaker of the "divine" life and holiness of God, and of the eternal priesthood of Christ. Indeed the saints of the past experienced a *divine holiness*, though not in the same degree or state as those who, in recent years, have experienced a greater outpouring of holiness through the gift of "living" in God's Will, which is best described as an *eternal holiness*. The eternal holiness of God perfects and fulfills the divine holiness that Christians receives at Baptism.

1.13 Consecration to Luisa

Controversy also surrounds the "consecrating" of oneself to the Servant of God Luisa.

Although the Church has not expressly discouraged consecrating oneself to Luisa, it directs our attention to the question, "What exactly do we intend by consecrating ourselves to Luisa?" and to the very words of consecration themselves. Suffice it to say that the Church has expressly prohibited certain forms of consecration. In a letter sent to the Holy See dated December 1, 1977, Cardinal Joseph Hoffner, Archbishop of Cologne and President of the German Episcopal Conference, requested an examination of a Pious Association within the Catholic Church dedicated to the work of the holy angels. The Congregation for the Doctrine of Faith, headed by Cardinal Ratzinger, affirmed that various forms of consecrations to the angels practiced in the Association are prohibited. We must keep this in mind when using certain forms of consecration that the Church has not approved or acknowledged, and we must always submit our judgment to the Church in this matter.

Let us remember that devotion to Luisa cannot be placed on the same level as devotion to Christ or to Mary. Although Luisa was the "*little* daughter of the Divine Will", and the secretary of the Holy Spirit's Fiat of Sanctification, we should be ready to die for Christ *before* Luisa. The misplacement of devotion to Luisa has led some to nurture and promote an unhealthy infatuation in regard to her person and her private revelations, and to neglect the reading of Sacred Scripture and participation in the Church's liturgical life, in particular the frequent reception of the Sacraments of the Holy Eucharist and of Penance.

1.14 Relics of Luisa

Another ambiguous teaching affirms that Luisa's relics "touched the divinity."

If this assertion is predicated on the assumption that since the Real Presence of Jesus abided in Luisa from one Holy Communion to the next, the contact of her body to such clothing or articles rendered them divine, this is not sound Catholic doctrine. For the mere contact of an article or material object with Luisa's human body does not translate into direct contact with the divinity of God. On the other hand, if this assertion is predicated on the affirmation that Luisa or her clothes touched Christ (i.e., during apparitions), one merely identifies Luisa's apparitions with the scores of seers throughout the centuries who also enjoyed apparitions of Christ, without presuming that such articles or clothing produce grace. To make such a presumption is to elevate an article to the level of a sacrament, and this is not sound Catholic doctrine.

Furthermore, while the term "relic" may be extended to the body and to the effects of a Servant of God and a Venerable for whom there is an official process, such relics cannot be freely marketed for a profit. Canon Law 1190 strictly forbids the sale of sacred relics. First-class relics are pieces of a saint's bone or flesh and are the most sacred. Second-class relics are objects a holy person wore or owned and are also highly valued. Third-class relics are items that have touched other relics and can be found in many church gift shops. It is worth noting that there is always the possibility of fakes being passed off as the real thing. Most relics when originally issued are accompanied by a document of authentication warranting the veneration of the relic. When relics are obtained from Church sources a "donation" is usually asked to cover the cost of the theca (the metal container) and manual labor, and this is relatively cheap. A donation is simply to cover costs, and anything more is not a donation – it is for a profit, and it is a violation of Church law, otherwise known as Simony.

In light of the above, those who replace the Crucifix or the Cross of Christ with Luisa's relic on the premise that Christ's Fiat of Redemption is inferior to the Spirit's Fiat of Sanctification, violate Catholic doctrine. The gift of Living in the Divine Will that Luisa received for the good of the Church does not do away with the Church's traditional symbols, devotions and customs, but complements and perfects them.

1.15 Luisa and the Saints

Another false teaching affirms that those who seek to live in the Divine Will must avoid praying or cultivating devotion to saints that existed before Luisa, as these possessed a holiness that is inferior to that of Luisa, and are therefore less capable of assisting us from heaven.

This affirmation is inconsistent with the Catholic Church's view of the efficacy of the merits and prayers of her canonized saints, whom she equally extols for their heroic virtues and sacrificial conquests. If the Church confers particular titles upon certain saints that correspond to their missions begun on earth, this is so these very saints may aid us in our missions on earth.

Thus the Church confers upon Ss. Benedict, Catherine of Siena and Bridget the title Patron of Europe, to whom God entrusts the continent of Europe and, in particular, those inhabitants who turn to them in prayer. The Church (Pope Pius XII) conferred on Our Lady of Guadalupe the title Patroness of the Americas, likewise entrusting to her the continents of North and South America and, in particular, those inhabitants who turn to her in prayer. The Church also gives us the patron of workers (St. Joseph), of preachers (St. John Chrysostom), of seminarians (St. Charles Borromeo), of confessors (St. John Vianney), even of the mentally ill (St. Dymphna), and so on. These patrons are given to us to aid us in our corresponding ministries and missions on earth. Certainly we can turn to Luisa or to any other saint to aid us in any undertaking or enterprise, but we must not denigrate or demean the efficacy of the prayers of the Church's saints simply because they came before Luisa and did not receive the gift of Living in the Divine Will. After all, Luisa prayed to St. Joseph and to other saints.[28] Let us not forget that in heaven "all" saints live in the Divine Will, and their prayers from above are vested with the efficacy and the effects of the Divine Will!

Moreover, God's gift to the Church of those saints whose bodies remained incorrupt bears witness to the eminent degree of their holiness that continually increases in heaven, and reminds us to turn to them in prayer. This miraculous legacy of posthumous incorruptibility is something that not even Luisa enjoyed, nor can she replace – at the exhumation of her body, Luisa was found corrupt. This gift of incorruptibility is one that God gives to whom He wills and why He wills. Also, in the approved prophetic revelations contained in the publication, *An Unpublished Manuscript on Purgatory* that bears that Church's *nihil obstat* and *imprimatur*, one

---

[28] Cf. message April 21, 1899.

discovers that the prayers of the souls in purgatory are sometimes more efficacious than the prayers of the saints in heaven.

1.16 Divine Will Asceticism

Another teaching error affirms that in the Divine Will the need for sacrifice is no longer necessary. Those who maintain this teaching assert that God's one Act unites and universalizes all human acts, thus rendering them "equal" in value. As a result, every action performed in the Divine Will – from pleasure to sacrifice – pleases God equally, as all acts are of equal objective value. Therefore, the human creature's sacrifices and mortifications are not of greater value than its consolations and pleasures: To eat a piece of candy and to fast in the Divine Will are one and the same thing so long as they are performed in the Divine Will.

This teaching deviates from the Church's ascetical and spiritual traditions that affirm that the human creature's sacrifices purify, dispose and perfect the soul in a way that pleasures or consolations do not. The ancient and traditional concepts of holocaust, oblation, atonement, expiation and sacrifice are ordered to the removal of sin and its effects from the individual and from the community, and to purify, dispose and sanctify both. To affirm that eating a piece of candy is equivalent to fasting for love of God and neighbor is to misplace the purpose and ends of sacrifice. While all of the human creature's acts – from sacrifice to pleasure – may be performed in the same spirit of Christian love and gratitude, they are not objectively equal acts, nor are their ends equivalent in value.

1.17 Sign of the Cross

Another false practice involves the replacing of the Church's traditional Sign of the Cross, "In the name of the Father, and of the Son and of the Holy Spirit," with the novel sign of the cross, "In the name of the Father, and of the Son and of Luisa."

This false practice constitutes a radical departure from the early teachings of the Apostles and the Church Fathers, and nullifies the indivisibility and unity of the three Divine Persons, the validity of Baptism, Penance and other Sacraments whose Trinitarian canonical form (along with matter) renders them valid.

1.18 Manichaeism

Another modern Divine Will teaching error threatens to revive the ancient heresy of **Manichaeism**, which affirms: "Marriage is an inferior state of sanctity, and the marital act of sexual union is an improper or imperfect expression of marital love." Some promoters are reported to have affirmed that before original sin Adam and Eve brought Cain and Abel into being without the procreative act, since physical generation was a sin and physical maternity a calamity. According to this false view, in the beginning God intended that Adam and Eve magically materialize Cain and Abel into existence through pious gazing at each other.

This approach is not sound Catholic doctrine, as the Book of Genesis reveals the goodness of the marital union before original sin (Gen. 1.28), and several early Church fathers affirm that the marital sexual union is intrinsically good. To affirm that the original procreative act was a sin is to affirm that all subsequent marital procreative acts are sinful or consequences of original sin, and this is contrary to Church teaching. Furthermore, in the Church-approved writings of the modern mystic Venerable Conchita de Armida who was a mother of nine children, Conchita affirms: "Being a wife and a mother was never an obstacle to my spiritual life." Speaking as a woman to one of her daughters-in-law, she added: "I have been very happy with my husband." And the Lord Himself told her one day: "You married in view of My great designs for your personal holiness, and to be an example for many souls who think that marriage is incompatible with holiness."

1.19 Monothelitism

Another Divine Will teaching error relates to the ancient heresy of **Monothelitism**, which affirms: "When you receive the gift of Living in the Divine Will, the human will ceases to operate, for God so totally absorbs, fuses and melts the human will within his own Divine Will that there remains only one operating will, only one active will in you, the Divine Will."

This heresy has been squelched in recent years thanks to the positive intervention of Church authorities, who have shown that when a soul lives in the Divine Will, both the human will of the creature and the Divine Will of God operate distinctly but not separately, in one accord.

May these clarifications regarding modern Divine Will teaching errors help all of you to abide in the truth, as you continue to enter ever-more deeply into the gift of Living in the Divine Will. Never forget that Living in the Divine Will is compatible with "all" devotions: it does not demean them, it does not denigrate them, but it elevates and perfects them through the *continuously eternal activity* of the three Divine Persons at work in you. I pray that unity may abound among the promoters of the Divine Will and among its devotees, who one day will join hands in reciting the *Our Father* prayer. Please remain obedient to the teachings of the Church, "speak the truth in charity" (Eph. 4.15), and above all love one another as children of the one Father who unites all things in Christ!

CHAPTER II

The Four Easy Steps to Living In The Divine Will

To prepare oneself for the mystical gift of Living in the Divine Will, it is fitting that we should explore the steps leading up to it. Earlier I gave evidence to support the reception of this gift through God's *continuously eternal activity* in the soul of the human creature that brings the past, present and future to a single point in God's eternal Act. Now, for all practical purposes, I show that it is quite simple to receive this gift through four easy steps: These steps are as follows: 1) *desire*; 2) *knowledge*; 3) *growth in virtue*; 4) *life*.

Step 1: Desire

In the approved writings of the Church's mystics Jesus makes it abundantly clear that *desire* is the most important ingredient to *enter into* and to *live in* God's Divine Will. Since it is ultimately the Holy Spirit that enables the human creature to desire and to correspond to God's Will, *knowledge* of his will occupies an ancillary role. Let us take for example the particular knowledge of Luisa Piccarreta's writings on the Divine Will. Although the knowledge of Luisa's writings is valuable, it does not per se *actualize* the Divine Will in the soul of the human creature. One can glean from the magisterial documents that the Spirit of God actualizes his gifts in the soul of human creature. Certainly knowledge of the inspired writings of Luisa and other recent mystics occupies an important role in the penetration and development of God's gifts, but without *desire*, such knowledge is of little or no value. It is only when the soul, literate or illiterate, learned or unlearned *desires* to live in God's Will that the entrance to the new mystical way has taken place. And as the soul more earnestly desires to live in God's Will, the more his will unfolds, where time and eternity unify in the sanctification of mankind and the entire cosmos. Living in the Divine Will is a mystical phenomenon that sometimes surpasses human sensory experience and eternally unifies the creature with the Creator. Jesus tells Luisa all that is required to obtain the gift of Living in the Divine Will is that the human creature offer its will entirely to God with a firm *desire*:

> While I was thinking about the Holy Divine Will, my sweet Jesus said to me: "My daughter, to enter into My Will there are neither paths, nor doors, nor keys, because My Will is found everywhere. It runs beneath the feet, to the right and to the left, over the head, everywhere. The creature does nothing other than remove the pebble of her will... This is because the pebble of her will impedes My Will from flowing in her... If the soul removes the pebble of her will, *in that same instant* she flows in Me, and I in her. She finds all of My goods at her disposition: light, strength, help, and all that she wants. That is why there are neither paths, nor doors, nor keys. *It is enough that she desires it, and everything is done!*"[29]

---

[29]   Luisa Piccarreta, *Pro-manuscripts* (Milano, Italy: Assocazione del Divin Volere, 1977); February 16, 1921.

Step 2: Knowledge

The particular knowledge we encounter in the writings of recent mystics on Living in the Divine Will attracts and disposes the human creature to a continuous, transforming union with God. Yet what directly motivates, actualizes, and perpetuates the human will in God's Will is the *Holy Spirit*, the sanctifier, who, attracted by our *desire*, "helps us in our weakness" by pleading in us "with sighs too deep for words." I here recall St. Augustine's teaching:

> There is then within us a kind of *instructed ignorance*, instructed, that is, by the Spirit of God who helps our weakness... the Apostle said:... "the Spirit helps us in our weakness; *we do not know what it is right to pray for, but the Spirit himself pleads with sighs too deep for words. He who searches hearts knows what the Spirit means, for he pleads for the saints according to God's will... he does it to enable you to know.*[30]

Undoubtedly particular knowledge is an effective *means* to attract and dispose us to Live in the Divine Will, but the absence of such knowledge does not keep us from experiencing this magnificent gift. And this is good news! By the power of the Holy Spirit who prays, sighs and pleads in the souls of the faithful, we can immediately receive the *desire* to obtain whatever gifts God wishes to grant us, in particular, the gift of the Divine Will. Now, the more we grow in the *knowledge* of God's gifts, the more we can appreciate them, correspond

---

[30]   St. Augustine, From a letter to bishop Proba; *Liturgy of the Hours* (NY: Catholic Book Pub. Co., 1975) Vol. IV, p.430.

to them and live them. In this sense, knowledge is an integral means and ingredient to Living in the Divine Will.

Step 3: Virtue

In order for the creature to "Live" in God's Divine Will, that is to remain in it without ever leaving, the creature must perfect its *desire continuously*. To do this, it sets out to inform its mind with sound spiritual teaching that will foster a greater awareness of God's Will, which will, in turn, set its will ablaze with love for him and for all creation. As the creature draws continuous enlightenment from God's revealed word, it seeks to prove its love in exchange for all that God has bestowed on it by continuous confirmations of desire. The creature confirms its desire through the development of the Christian virtues. Here we encounter the words of St. Hannibal di Francia, who captures the essential human ingredient for remaining in the Divine Will:

> In order to form, with this new science, saints who may surpass those of the past, the new Saints *must also have all the virtues, and in heroic degree, of ancient Saints* – of the Confessors, of the Penitents, of the Martyrs, of the Anachorists, of the Virgins, etc.[31]

Jesus confirms this teaching to Venerable Conchita:

> Once transformation into Jesus is brought about, the Holy Spirit also becomes the spirit of the creature raised to a more or less higher degree according to

---

[31]   Letters of St. Hannibal to Luisa Piccarreta, *Collection of Letters Sent by St. Hannibal Di Francia to the Servant of God, Luisa Piccarreta* (Jacksonville, Center for the Divine Will: 1997), letter n. 2.

the intensity and amplitude of transformation, *which strictly depends on the growth of the soul in virtue.*[32]

Hence the more one develops the Christian virtues the more the Divine Will expands in that individual. Needless to say, this stability in virtue is grounded in a lifestyle of prayer and work, like that of the saints of old. A life of prayer may include a varied form of pious practices such as meditation, spiritual reading, discursive and contemplative prayer, fasting, abstinence, which, in turn, compliment a life of work.

As the creature exchanges love with its Creator, no sooner does it realize its awfully *finite* character of love, than it turns to its Creator to take from him his *infinite* love that embraces heaven and earth and every act of every creature in time and in eternity, in order to fuse itself within his divine and eternal being. In this way the creature and the Creator form *one* synergetic action in two distinct but inseparable wills. And if the human creature's will remains free to break from God's eternal will to commit sin, its stability in God's divine virtue disposes it to refrain from doing so. The creature's virtues, under the influence of the Holy Spirit, have faithfully reared and trained it to *Live* in the Divine Will with a continuous respect and with a holy fear.

Step 4: Life

The more the union of wills increases between Creator and creature, the more graces and wonders the creature discovers while advancing in unending degrees of holiness. The advancement in one single degree of holiness is a new

---

[32]   Marie Michel Philipon, O.P., *Conchita: A Mother's Spiritual Diary* (New York: Alba House, 1978) p. 230.

life of grace that only eternity can fathom – so incredible is its achievement. It is the life of the blessed internalized on earth ordered to exponential growth. To *Live* in the Divine Will is to live eternity on earth, it is to mystically traverse the present laws of time and space, it is the human soul's ability to simultaneously trilocate into the past, the present and the future, while influencing every act of every creature and fusing them in God's eternal embrace! Initially most souls will often enter and exit the Divine Will until they arrive at *stability in virtue.* Yet it is this stability in divine virtue that will help them to participate *continuously* in the Divine Will, which defines *Living* in the Divine Will.

As for the date of our permanent entry in the Divine Will, though God seldom reveals this date to his creatures, he reassures us that at the moment when we possess a continuously 'upright intention' and 'firm desire' to live in his will, that is by all standards the most fitting day when we Live in the Divine Will.

May we strive to live the greatest gift God has given humankind in these days preceding the universal era of peace. May we immerse ourselves in God's eternal life in order to become Living Tabernacles of the Eucharistic Jesus. It is a gift that is ours for the asking, and all we have to do is *desire it, know it, grow in its virtue, and live it.*

Fiat!

About the Author

Rev. Joseph L. Iannuzzi is a theologian and doctoral alumnus of the Gregorian Pontifical University. As a former freestyle and greco-roman wrestler, Fr. Iannuzzi pursued postgraduate studies in biology, philosophy and theology at seven universities in North America and in Europe. He has translated six theological works from Italian to English, and he was an associate exorcist of Fr. Gabriel Amorth, the exorcist of Rome.

Fr. Joseph is member of the missionary religious community located in the Diocese of Marquette, MI that enjoys the ecclesiastical approval of the local bishop and the added endorsements of two bishops of the Detroit Diocese. As an international association that promotes the Church's mystical tradition, the missionary community provides solo-wilderness retreats at the CCL (Companions of Christ the Lamb) spiritual center that spans well over 1,000 acres of verdure in the village of Paradise, MI. Those interested in making solo-wilderness retreats to deepen their union with God's Divine Will may contact Fr. Joseph, P.O.Box 12, Paradise, MI 49768.

Fr. Joseph is presently completing a dissertation on the writings and doctrines of the Servant of God Luisa Piccarreta at the Pontifical University of Rome. He is the author of five books on mystical and dogmatic theology, the initiator of international Divine Will communities and instructor on the proper theological presentation of the mystical gift of *Living in God's Divine Will*.

Additional Resources by Rev. Joseph Iannuzzi!

THE TRIUMPH OF GOD'S KINGDOM IN THE MILLENNIUM AND END TIMES

This authoritative book provides solid answers on one of the most confusing but important topics today. Demonstrates the reality of God's Kingdom on earth where Christ will reign but not in the flesh. Based solely on Scripture, Fathers and Doctors of the Church, and approved Church teachings, this book is a one-of-a kind treasure.   **$ 14.95 + $3.95 s/h**

THE SPLENDOR OF CREATION

In this groundbreaking book, theologian Fr. Joseph Iannuzzi discusses a period of time in the not-to-distant future that many Christians eagerly await—the coming era of peace known as the Millennium. Written from a scholarly, theological perspective, the Splendor of Creation is readable, well documented, and highly informative. The figurative thousand-year era of peace that is foretold in the twentieth chapter of St. John's book of Revelation is the subject of this work.
$ 19.95 + $3.95 s/h

ANTICHRIST AND END TIMES

Today, as the world sinks deeper into moral depravity and intellectual confusion, talk of the Antichrist's rise again fills the air. Christian leaders believe this is because the signs of his coming—heresy, apostasy, and iniquity—have reached unparalleled levels. This powerful book, takes a hard look at the prophecy, its history, and the conditions necessary to bring about its fulfillment, offering readers a unique glimpse at an eschatological mystery rooted in the book of Revelation.   **$ 18.00 + $3.95 s/h**

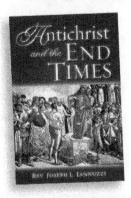

CPSIA information can be obtained
at www.ICGtesting.com
Printed in the USA
BVOW11s2026030518

515184BV00001B/77/P

9 781891 903359